South × South

South × South

Poems from Antarctica

Charles Hood

OHIO UNIVERSITY PRESS

ATHENS

Ohio University Press, Athens, Ohio 45701
ohioswallow.com
© 2013 by Charles Hood

To obtain permission to quote, reprint, or otherwise reproduce or distribute material
from Ohio University Press publications, please contact our rights and permissions
department at (740) 593-1154 or (740) 593-4536 (fax).

Printed in the United States of America
Ohio University Press books are printed on acid-free paper ⊗ ™

23 22 21 20 19 18 17 16 15 14 13   5 4 3 2 1

Library of Congress Cataloging-in-Publication Data
Hood, Charles, 1959–
  South x South : poems from Antarctica / Charles Hood.
     pages cm
  Includes bibliographical references.
  ISBN 978-0-8214-2038-6 (pbk. : acid-free paper) — ISBN 978-0-8214-4455-9
(electronic)
  1. Antarctica—Poetry. I. Title.
  PS3558.O538S68 2013
  811'.54—dc23

                        2012045764

Contents

North, south, east, and west run the lines. A fence, a farm road, a row of trees, the tight streets of a sleepy county seat, a uniquely American graffiti. Only in the sky can we emerge from these surroundings to discover the scale of the experiment that has been worked upon us.

—William Langewiesche, *Inside the Sky*

Food for the Moon

Good place to meet dead people,
Antarctica. White like a hospital. *Go fetch that colored nurse,*
she's nicer than the others. My father died saying it was late,
dinner was over, he was going to get up and bang
out the dishes, forgetting he was dead
give or take a day or two already.

He always did like taking trips. Now I show him the map,
pressing it facedown on the grass so he can read it without
his glasses. It is British and nicely printed. Here is the dirigible
mooring mast and here is the pioneer cemetery. Here is the sea ice.
Here is the place between the scratches in the light
where I will go to line up with the men

> who wear wooden slits for masks,
> who know how to eat seals,
> who mush dogs and mend leather,

who even after the outside parts of their bodies turn black
and stiff will still ski to the moon on ivory blades
made from their own hand-carved teeth.

Waking Up with Mechanics

Do the same extras drive the cars in my dreams each night, or do they work in shifts? There can't be more than forty or fifty cars; maybe they all come from a central lot, are shared out among us. Maybe that is why they drive so well. Somewhere between Christchurch and McMurdo I wake up in a web seat inside an Air Force C-17 in time to hear somebody say that when it comes down to it, you can use urine to rinse off just about anything.

And somebody else insists, no, not Wednesdays, it's Thursdays that the condom bowl is refilled in 155, and all I know is that I already ate my lunch

and it's not time to get up and put on our Big Reds,

and in one of the dreams there was a car sort of like the 1957 Bel Air my grandfather had, two-toned turquoise and cream, and wouldn't it be cool to airlift one of those down to McMurdo and put on whitewalled snow tires and just to drive slowly up and down the gravel and ice of Highway One, lip-synching 1940s-era Tommy Dorsey and Frank Sinatra, the only car without an emergency kit and a serial number for a thousand miles?

C-17, *Pegasus Field*

To land, a verb, meaning to blink a lot
and to use a Gomer Pyle outside voice
while still inside the plane. *Sha-zaam.*

Did I know that 300 feet of 29-degree saltwater
churning under 100 feet of cantilevered ice-ledge

covered by 30 feet of secondhand snow tamped
tight like a kind of paste made from cornflakes
painted white is all that's holding

up this 200-ton C-17 that once carried Shamu
the crew chief asks.

I did not. Thank you. White

bunny boots like two Ls of burn-ward gauze. My head
has become a fat moon

in a small sky. Now he waves at a mouth
of light

and all the red angels behind you moan and push
and another angel on the ice windmills

like Pete Townsend and you stare down at the backlit ladder
between here and there thinking,
please don't let me fall down.
It is so white and perfect and all

it seems impossible not to hold onto the doorway
a little longer while agreeing with Keats:

better if we were butterflies

and liv'd
but three summer days.

Tulips

Bill and Liza have divorced—in the Crary Lab I am reading about gentoo penguins—but Darby and Joan hang in there, as do all of the extended Ash-Dumps. It just sounds like something out of *The Honeymooners*. Johnnycakes wanders alone, uncertain. That little bastard Archie has a nest of hundreds of stones, ten times more than he needs, yet still steals constantly—the more abject the nest, the more he takes. Of the south side, only Leo is worse. Herbert intrudes on Horace and Alice; after a long day of battles, Alice goes off with Herbert to the site past the dump. Kinky or just curious, one still without a name favors necrophilia and will not leave the dead research specimens alone.

It makes me want to go back to school, become a post-doc, get a grant and come back here, just so I can name all of my study penguins after tulips. Candlelight (I will write) is a sport of Lucky Strike with better form even than Peer Gynt. Bestseller, Parade, Burning Love, Monte Carlo—of these, what more can be said? They died for science. Easter Surprise is a Tango that looks like a Rembrandt; yesterday he ate 22% more krill by weight and volume than Dreamboat, Cum Laude, or Zampa Rose. Black Hero joins Queen of the Night in the maroon-black void of deep water, a negative hole in the colony until they struggle back into the garden. Who noted the first eggs laid by Fringed Beauty? Cum Laude is a Single Late now that the Darwins have reorganized. We all have our parts in the passion: wing-tagged skuas rogue the distressed and the ill. Goya looks bad tonight. Harried and worn out, the Hocus Pocus clan loses feathers mid-rise. Some families will thrive, like Puget Sound and Olympic Flame, whose males preen and glow, fresh from the water. A vigorous form of Double Late, Uncle Tom's demand climbs steadily, while Ted Turner could win a medal at a show, he has such good posture.

Murillo barks *he-haw* with joy. Skuas pass and feint, then give up on Greigii, so perfectly black-backed he flares green and bronze. Maybe tomorrow or the day after Dreamboat will be snatched by a leopard seal, but today he stands on Alta Vista, ecstatic and tall, muddy footprints running like tan valentines up and down her back. We all want to be Dutch Triumphs. A row of clean, dark brown dirt waits behind the shorefast second-year ice. Clouds curl and lift. The sun on the upraised beak of Dreamboat makes it look like he is reaching for the sky one final time, and this time, if Alta will stay just a little bit more still, he is sure he will make it.

Things the Doctor Asks

That is an interesting scar,
were you an especially clumsy child?

Count backwards from one hundred
in multiples of pi. Hold out both hands.

If you die, may we cremate you?
Why does my stethoscope transmit

a dim hum like a hive of bees?
Now get dressed. You mean

you are not dressed yet even
after all this time? Shut up

and stop counting. Open the door.
You will need Diamox, for the Pole.

You will need to shave those parts.
Do you know that you walk around

like a hut with legs?

Girl, Trees, Paper Balloons

1783: How quiet and still the people on the ground
seemed, said the first people to rise

in balloons. Quiet as milk. Somewhere the son
of the son of the son of the man who was the last person to let go
of the line so the first balloon could be free of us
is lighting a cigarette. Heaven is a movie—
even the audience smokes Lucky Strikes.

They have a box there for my memories and in case I burn up
in the light like a faulty meteor I have given them two or three things

to keep such as my mother's saddle oxfords and the one about
the man described in the newspaper who was dead for three days

in the ocean but woke up, alive, and the one about when the snow
in moonlight was whiter than washing machines behind the dump,

and the one playing now, the one
with woodwinds rising as maples seedpod
the tattoos on the slim shoulders of the girl
kissing me like my mouth is a parachute

just about to open.

Last Year's Checklist

Where are the goggles that protect against magic?

Am I married? Do I have children?
They ask but I do not remember. Yes—

no. Sure. I am practicing how to spit penguins
out of my head like black seeds. Grappa

blurs the Chileans, not later at McMurdo
but before, Rey Jorge, where church is Mexican

blue shipping containers, three pews
and a plugged-in Mary.

Are you my mother
I want to ask the Russian soup

ladle woman with the gold front tooth.
Can *you* explain it? Oswaldo, laughing,

va va va-vooms his jacket off for her
and pushes his fingers through the cigarette

burns in the chest of his long johns.
He is a mountaineer and paints maps

so he must know why two burned-out Soviet
tanks mirror rust in the puddles of the airfield

but he jumps lenses and escapes just as the patriotic
tuba music of the Motherland fills the dining room

and my heart turns into a bundle
of sparrows and my hands push past

zippers trying to reach in and tuck them
all back into their red folds,

telling them just wait, people are watching,
we will fly around the room later.

I Take Good Notes, Getting Ready to Fly South

An airship or dirigible is a type of aerostat. An aerostat is a type of lighter-than-air aircraft. An aircraft is a kind of bowtie worn by the sky to piss off lakes and swamps, dirt, center-pivot-irrigation, forest fires. Aerostatic aircraft stay aloft by heating gas slowly, over a burner, then using a tube to blow it into shapes, a swan, even a unicorn, what girls like before they like the flammability of boys. The history of flight mostly has to do with blood and ice. No, the history of flight in Antarctica can't be told just now, it is mostly too sad for this time of night, but for example there were once two pilots, I met them in a bar in McMurdo,

and the first one was telling the second one, shit, I had to turn back. The other one said, well what for. First one, well my hair was on fire. Second one said, I hate when that happens.

Scale Model

Maybe just marine-grade plywood with tar balls
and kerosene: if bursts of fire come in matchboxes,
what kind of holder does Antarctica come in?

Draw this abyss,
art school: make me
a mold of France—all of France—then cast it in white resin.

Set it beside a 1-to-1 replica of Greenland.
Only two hundred more pieces of the basement
railroad still to go.

Marble Point Refueling Station

It all comes at us so hard
to remember, beauty. At lunch

I study the fuel tech, how her face burned
clean by the wind matches her hands

outside of her folded work gloves,
hands like a kind of telegram

saying *you would die for this*.
I will sleep in the freezer

attached to a kind of pipe,
will pee in the funnel welded

onto the barrel, will try not
to explain at breakfast how

by being there she makes me
wince three or four times

a minute. I want to write to
somebody in charge, say, *go easy,*

we're new. Later after dinner
I ask about the dog

star, what night here looks
like at night. She won't

say, but when I ask
what she likes best about

being here, she smiles,
looks away, looks back—

the tilt.

The History of Luck

Some ancient penguins were red. Today one kind of penguin lives in abandoned houses in Namibia, standing around like people at a wedding. Others, for example in the Chathams, burrow like shy, dark thumbs. Who knows why one is one and one is not. In the late 1950s an American geologist in Antarctica walked away from four plane crashes in a row. That becomes stupid, like somebody hit by lightning twice, once raising his left hand, once his right.

Stepping from his second wreck Hemingway said, *my luck, she eeez running very good.*

My plane was hit by lightning in Costa Rica once, buck and swerve as the cabin lights surged on and off. What is luck, is it a kind of underwear you put on before a date, is it being born you and not your brother? We are all lucky because some lemur long ago remembered to evolve gorgeous amber eyes. We are lucky that our parents' parents survived smallpox, dengue fever, being raped by Cossacks, crossing the flooded plank by groping with a numb boot in the muddy brown water beneath which the tops of drowned trees waved like dead hands, survived bear maulings and influenza, caesarian sections with a jackknife and a swig of vodka, survived the long absences when the father of the grandfather of the grandfather joined the sealers and was gone for three years at a go, his hands so cold on the rigging he thought he would never touch the deck, try pots boiling over, beatings for insubordination, the time the ship went aground, then, just as suddenly, washed back off of the reef, the time he survived being robbed in Brazil, survived scurvy and tetanus and not being able to brush his own teeth after his hands were burned one year, survived being stabbed by a gaff hook when pitch and roll reversed themselves, survived boredom and fear and the month of dark nights when suicide sat in his belly like hunger, we are lucky because fins became hands and hands became nimble enough to flamenco the guitar strings and win prizes, win bets, win hearts, hearts that we are lucky now to have as well because no matter how many times people stab us in them and no matter how often the lightning strikes the people next to us, we still know that it won't hit us, it can't hit us, not even in the middle of all this ice—after all, look how lucky we always are.

Manifest for a Pole Flight

Some days you wake up so tired

you want somebody else to hold the strings,
hay foot, straw foot,

help you walk.

What's-To-Eat-Today on the chow hall's
whiteboard has just a one-word entry:
        C A T F O O D .

Eat your catfood, finish your coffee, bus your tray, dress
like an Eskimo pretending to be a North Face ad, walk to the lab,
touch the dead penguin for luck, take a good close-up picture
of the crabs in their tank. Check to see if the meteorites
have come in. Check email. Yes, you can go,
it says, but you have to sing. Sing what.
Oh anything will do. *Send me north,*
send me south, send me to be a gold
tooth in the penguin king's mouth.

Yes, all right. You can go.

Free-Fall (1)

Cause of death: optimism and miscalibration,
optimism and euphoria and 300 feet of snow
pancaked on top of 9,000 feet of glacial ice. Optimism.

On the Herc flight to the Pole they tell me about the skydivers.

Died in the free-fall position, some of them punching snow angels
six feet deep.

Free-Fall (2)

Skydivers at the South Pole: watches must have had the wrong altimeter settings—at each side of the world, north and south, life and death, the air stretches and thins, distorts, gives out false readings like a tarot deck that tells only lies. They had not even pulled ripcords. So high they had no air to breathe, no air to brace against, falling, going faster than at sea level, faster than clock hands spinning. Could they hear it? It is like a simple word problem in math: the first 1,000 feet will take approximately 10 seconds and then you will fall 1,000 feet every 5 seconds. So a free fall from 10,000 feet up will take 30 seconds, true or false. Falling through air into a field of air perhaps they smiled, happy to see how slowly time was passing, perhaps not even surprised when they realized how little time it takes when you are made out of wax to become the blue flame and not the yellow one.

What Comes Next

When you crash at the South Pole (Frank Capra, *Dirigible*, 1931) these things happen
your friends die. You go blind. Your wife wants to leave you. You push a sled
for a month and end up just going in a circle, back to the original graves.
None of these is the bad thing.

The bad thing is that the only way home after you crash your plane at the South Pole
is by begging to be rescued by that most ass-smeared of airships,

a dirigible.

Our Lady of Sorrow.

Some things cannot be fixed, even with strapping tape and wing dope.

One was named June —

that was the copilot, Harold June. Ashley McKinley,
photographer. Pilot, Bernt Balchen. So bad to cross

Byrd. Raw winds blew from him. He named mountains,
even the ones he had not seen. He burned

the diaries of those he did not trust. When Byrd
was flown over the Pole in 1929 — he did not fly over

but was flown over — he said, just loud enough,
about fucking time. Pee bottles rolling back and up,

pencils, a broken thermos. Sandwich paper
balled like baby fists. Rough landings on ice.

He did not help pour. He haloed his face
in wolf fur, center of every lens,

center of yellow orchids
of ego. When Byrd was flown over

the Pole he knew from then on
somebody would always have to say,

in a restaurant or at a filling station
or the congressional hearing,

Look, there he is.

A Short History of Flight with an Emphasis on Food

Icarus, of course. Flatbread
in the cover leaking a bead

Da Vinci wanted to glide
much thought

past care
now as would

and what about
the whole bottle

up over the sides.
spread them on the table.

This one lost synchronization
stalled, landed on the flat top

and restarted halfway down.
in the chubby Chianti bottles.

into each brown photograph.
In training this one was rolled

iron grocery stall shooting
how to hit. This one has

had his joystick push right
air, in the cockpit, makes

trench expression, *hoosh*—

wrapped in grape leaves, a small wound
of olive oil up and down the wet seam.

for hours, he dreamed it, drew it, had not
about where to put the skin for wine

for worries like that, just wanted to go
you, any of us, if we were honest

World War I, sandwiches and usually
taken up, and when empty, one throws

By then we have the photographs, can
This one hanged himself after the war.

and shot his propeller in two. This one
of a dirigible, coasted the length, rolled off,

Loaves of bread, cheese. Candles like corks
This one has three dogs, enjoys getting them

This one is sad. This one lied about his age.
up and down tracks inside a kind of wheeled,

at paper-on-wood silhouettes he never did learn
received the *Légion d'honneur*; once in a crash

through his jaw. This one is you. The rushing
it so hard to breathe it feels like drowning. A

just a heated tin of snow, lard, bully beef, hard

tack. Whatever's at hand.   Every morning Scott after losing the Pole

still had to help make hoosh.   Before that, 1902, Antarctica's first balloon flight:
Scott went as high as the rope   stretched tight allowed but on the whole Scott

did not approve. Like a sow   playing the piano or lines of women voting,
it was not natural. If not snow   dead he would have been taken up two years

later in the Great War and all   the others with him. Just simple math. To
fly only makes it come sooner.   This one weighs the same as a jockey.

This one they sang over softly.   This one's hands are kneading something
warm in a towel and if you just   wait a second he will walk back with you.

Robert Falcon Scott Strikes-Through
His Journal Coming Back from the Pole

His friends called him Con; the men, The Owner.
At Scott's memorial service even the King prayed.

They all wrote then—letters, plays, diaries—even the
scabs and pickets. Even Cap⁺ Scott dead in his tent

kindly numbered his journals, and, inside the front
cover of No. 3, wrote this:

Diary can be read by finder to ensure recording of Records, &c.,
but Diary should be sent to my widow.

And on the first page:

Send this diary to my ~~wife~~ widow. R. SCOTT.

Matchbox

1.

Randy was eleven. I was five. He and I had these cars from
England, Matchbox. It seemed the wrong word, *matchbox,*

because the neighbors smoked matches but in little folded-over packets.
Nana bought us a box of matches big as a paperback book. The pilot

light on the heater went out all the time. We used a lot of matches.
They were made of wood and got stuck out of reach behind

the faucet thing. Hot Wheels came later. Their wheels were
not hot and were not even wheels, just hollow plastic cups.

If you pulled them off sharp wires stuck out. The track sections
were orange as pop and when I asked my dad if somewhere

there were orange roads he told me to ask my mother
but she was busy with the matches so that was that.

2.

Everything interesting smelled like gas masks. You
could buy a bayonet, a parachute in Army Surplus.

My dad on weekends was building a shed out of two-by-fours
but it was always just the frame and we would tip it over,

cover it with dark green wool army blankets and Randy
gave me a Bedford Tipper because I let him touch me

until some of the parents found out and it was taken apart.
The blanket was used to clean some paint and then was

burned with the blue rags people used to change the oil.
Nobody ever talked about it.

Pemmican

Machine-rolled cigarettes. Hoppe's gun oil.
Food List, 1937:

biscuit	2.7	ounces per man per day
cocoa	0.8	"
oatmeal	2.0	"
pemmican	5.6	"
sugar	3.2	"
yeast	0.4	"
milk powder	1.6	"
margarine	5.6	"
pea flour	1.6	"

also, 1 capsule, reduced halibut oil
1 tablespoon, concentrate of orange juice
1 can sweetened condensed milk (on birthdays only)

Dibs on Shotgun

I want to name this view *Hundred Mile Joy Circle*.

Side trip to check the state of the pack ice; side trip
to Blood Falls. This part just here, pilot says,

is what we call Tornado Alley. Bad crash two
three years ago.

And me saying yes, roger that, thinking

we study art history to learn how to speak the languages of
the recently dead. To paint glaciers

first learn how to paint teeth.

Royal New Zealand Air Force

Waking up in old sheets,
old diaries. For example

1958: Royal NZ Air Force
plucky single-engine Auster Mk7c
had to be shipped back from Scott
Base near McMurdo back home to
Christchurch. The wings already
had been unbolted and set aside
but engine and prop still worked.

How to get it from A to B and how
cool to have seen it, since to get it to
the ship but without wings it was driven
along the ice shelf propeller running,
tail high, like a homemade swamp buggy
from some arctic version of the Everglades,
and insomuch as the fact was that then
a brace of dead alligators were all that
were missing pegged to each side of the
plane's olive drab cabin doors like foxtails
or some kind of reptile headlights.

Wrapped like take-home
burritos

engines in foil
waiting to be rescinded
home, bolted to a frame
cradle and strapped to a
decked hold. Wings first
now the engine and now care
even in the cold, end-of-season

finger-split work that says how
much of life is just about hunger
and epoxy. Glue the cut skin
back together with a dab of
resin, take a hit of backdoor
hootch, just get on with it.
In the wind it takes longer
to do anything, even pee,
penis strange to hands, hands
strange to arms, arms
steel angels of frozen light.

Galen Rowell Rides Eliot Porter Like a Pony

in Photography Heaven while An-My Lê
takes Polaroids of how their footsteps,
in the snow, run away like boats
that don't know yet they can't
be wild horses.

FSA

I share a room with an ice climber and somebody
from NASA. Their socks want to be with mine

and I say *no, no,* and kick them savagely. A woman
from Minneapolis sentences her shit-brindle sweater

to solitary confinement inside the dorm dryer, sets it on a cold cycle
for three days. So much for the rest of us. I have brought ten flutters

of Bounce in a quart Ziplock but when NASA pajamas asks,
I say I am out. Until the down-the-hall girls finish, no point

anyway. I hide the Ziplock between the pages of a book.
I am sure they had Wal-Mart and Target in his town

and he always forgets to lock the door.

Ben Shahn the FSA photographer swore it is true because he was
there: farmer was being rejected for a Dust Bowl loan. Something out
of *Grapes of Wrath,* and things are grim but not decided yet either
way. Farmer pleads. Banker says, Here's a sporting offer, old timer. If
you can guess which one of my eyes is a glass one, you can have your
loan. The farmer doesn't hesitate. "The left one." And of course he's
right—the banker says, *Holy Joe, how did you know?* Farmer, It's the
one that looked the kindest.

Telling Michael Light

about my friend the hole-
in-one golfer, we get on to sea-
planes, and how in the UK, to get certified,

one has to learn all the naval flag codes

including   *stay away*
                cholera on board.

Sunrise on Mercury

You go to the South Pole, think, okay, these people are all here because they don't want to be someplace else. Yet the future of people in Antarctica may be that there won't be any people. People are expensive. They sulk and in the Dry Valleys pee where they shouldn't. Some, like me, want to sleep with the cooks. The future of Antarctic aviation is probably drones, just wings and a camera joysticked out of a darkened room in Las Vegas. People are as useless as 1955 helicopter blades, though I look around and am sad to think some day all these rock jocks and f-stop guys and drag-bag Carhartt lost pilgrims with a pink Mohawk and a nose ring may have to get real jobs. Or else not: maybe they can ride it out, run a trap line in Montana, wait for the Antarctica that will come after this one. What is south of south? Sunrise on Mercury. Some day we will need fuel techs on the moon. There was a guy at Pole Station, I can't decide if he's tired or just walks like a marionette as we talk about Byrd's book *Alone* one night the same as day in the wide-windowed Galley: cage fighter thin, ponytail, askew beard, looks like a Forest Service smokechaser or the kind of guy who could have soloed Denali three times then gotten whacked up crazy bad on the fourth. Beneath the jeans, those feet. Can't tell if he's wearing really odd neoprene booties or if he's got artificial legs. Trying to hold eye contact while staring down *yes or no*

to find out.

Kate Coles Erases Me

or was that the other email   a mast breaks   (and so cut the sailor adrift
howling   rage seas in winter   a very tender part   not a problem

of course I *like* mailing things   as if shot from a gun and no
a skeet disk   buckshot chasing buckshot   rhymes with sleet

if there's to be any weather   think of them as hunched
even mechanized   not like a blond river of gazelles burning

fences   skimmering grass   that pitch / yaw thing   doing it with my hand
.sweeping down low   a pelagic dogfight of ballerinas   black pearls

in moonlight   collapses into what   the graphic, pre-ether
scalpel and wound   albatross cagefights shearwater next

to petrels   too hard for me   Spam and windmills   see *A Humument*
see the mast in Cambridge   an open-ocean hero boat   and then

or a bowsprit   absurdly important   an even colder rain   yet pointless
it may be too hard
                or perhaps just as good to

     and why not

The Suicide of Lawrence Oates

A skilled man can peel
fifty seals an hour. In sunshine a man may take his shirt off,
his drawers,

work naked. Snow
dry as sand. You can wash your hands in it.
He may show you lilac faces

on his arms, his back,
intersections where the nineteenth century
pushed into the twentieth

then sheared off.
Just try and dig the point out. Which is family,
which is horror show?

Fingers probe, lingering.
The last penguin-oil factory closed in 1919,
iron try pots skiltywibbled

like standing stones,
tumbled helmets for the dead kings
of Antarctica.

He rode in a cart, waving,
my father did, through the sugarcane on Guam.
White brides

the natives said,
loving the sailors on parade in their highwater
pants. Gilligan hats,

napkin-ring scarves,
strange sleeves and stripes: even the straight ones
looked taken queer.

Guam rails
on the B-29 runway, all extinct now, blame
introduced army snakes.

Funny how stray weeds
arrive innocent of any bad intention,
even in the senna,

dried for boot liners
and stuffed in bunches around the butter tins,
or sweet flock,

a medicine.
Price's Patent Belmont Stearine Candles
reeked of bad tallow

like a museum
of grandparents. What do you dream?
When the nails

came in kegs
it was worth two column inches
in Auckland papers. Machine-

made screws,
such a marvel. What next, mutton birds
that catch themselves? Screw

them into your arms,
your head. Be a peacock for machine love.
My father was a kind of love

machine
which had no fan belt, no drive chain.
You could run

your fingers around
his jawline, behind his head when he slept,
do it twenty times,

still never find the switch.
Back then men could offload dead seals like sacks of coal
all day and not mind.

Now we finger their shirts,
admiring how, unlike us, our tattoo-faced fathers
knew when it was time to leave,

when it was time to push
open the tent flap and step out,
turning to lean back

inside and say
as casually as possible *I am just going outside now
and may be some time*.

Briefing

Zoos had to get animals somewhere. Still trying to find out if it is true or not that Navy chopper pilots in the '50s, trying to touch down in a whiteout, dropped fluorescent tennis balls to see how far to the deck. Stories. Everybody lies about it now but just before they rotated home to the States, what is true is that turning pilots would set down fast on the shore ice, grab two or three penguins, shove them in a sack, gun it back to McMurdo, walk in late to the debriefing and throw up their hands, *who me?*

> *Something hinky in the fuel line so's I had to touch down*
> *but don't you worry I got that bitch hosed out clean.*

Meanwhile cargo's in a sealed tank by now, a fist of anchovies, grease pencil marks it *science*, zip back home, priority handling.

Sell every last one. San Francisco Zoo
filled an entire grotto this way.

Arrival Forms

Field notes on Satan in Antarctica: When he walks past a turned-off TV, it glows blue. Like a penguin's, his tongue is stiff, barbed. When stirred by more than usual lust, Satan shuffles and brays. Crinkled jazz eyes, red as grief. On the landing card at the airport under profession, he always writes in a small neat hand

as in the astronomical sense, I am a singularity.

Fifteen Seconds

Filming *Encounters at the End of the World* at McMurdo
Werner Herzog said,

> You think that this hurts but it doesn't. On *Fitzcarraldo*, in Peru,
> when the woodcutter was bitten by the snake, he knew that he would die,
> so he thought about it for maybe fifteen seconds, then with the chainsaw
>
> he cut off his own foot.

Morning Edition

The math is simple. Mt. Erebus
                        named for son of Chaos
is just under 13,000 feet tall.
                        but say Erebus to a geologist
                        it means piled lava stone ice
                        a big strange mountain and

The plane hit 11,500 feet below the summit, near
sea level, the Air New Zealand pilots thinking they
were still over the middle of McMurdo Sound.

                        say it to a navy history
                        book it means 1841

                        a ship the HMS Erebus,
                        captained south by Ross

                        naming seas and volcanoes

Wrong computer codes. They had the wrong authorization
sequence. The crash made the US papers even, 257 people,
all dead. I was writing a paper the day it happened

                        say Flight 901 to the rescue
                        crew trying to find the parts

                        camped months among
                        the burned fat with

                        skuas eating the corpses
                        their own food gone

snowed in, means

quoting the person who was saying how modern movies
are society's version of what we want the world to be like,
novels are our version of how it really is, and newspapers

> *you never will be*
> *the same again*

are a kind of misguided judge who tears the difference in half
right down the middle   *—and they were like canvas*

> *pharaohs how*
> *the old boys died*

> *they died in 1912*
> *like British men*

> *the old men*
> *died*

> *like boys*
> *playing camp-out*

> *the camp*
> *and its bodies*

> *touching too close*
> *to the perfect*

> *and the strange*
> *so the relief party*

> *just buried them*
> *there, in the tent*

of rocks that would be
as good a cairn or summit

as any. Where are they now,
the snow having built up

burying the burial snow
and that snow burying

the rest. Scott
moves downhill

eyes closed
hands still

holding the case
of his sextant

his sextant
on his chest

his chest on
its way to become

leather and
after leather

a moraine
and after

that a field
of hard white

stars
riding

like ice
on the wings

of Flight 901
forever.

Shackleton's Grave

will be moved from picket fence tourist whisky South
Georgia up into Shackleton Crater, spike of water ice & black
light at the South Pole of the moon, just as soon as I can find
my car keys
                          and a shovel whose handle ain't busted.

Some Luck, McMurdo

McMurdo has three bars. I am in the small brown one.

My date has white socks and a red henley burned
into my palms. So far I have won $100 at karaoke

and $200 playing *Warhammer*
and if this keeps up

I tell myself, pretty soon

you'll need sunglasses just to read
your mail.

Miss Gallagher

Today a Wednesday no it's Thursday Human Resources reports that
McMurdo is 28% women which is 2% above normal and which is
pretty good since I am only 80 or 90% male myself

and what would the First Ones say, Scott or Amundsen or Apsley
Cherry-Garrard, maybe they would say *about time* or *who will sew my
smalls* and in the no-women Cold War days there was 1962 at Scott
Base the self-contained Miss Gallagher

who wore a checked skirt khaki shirt flowered headscarf. Poor Miss
Gallagher had no fingers on her left hand and a broken nose. Arm
askew. Never quite sure where to look. But complete even so and
under the skirt the neutered nude parts had been unneutered or
maybe all mannequins back then came that way

and sometimes she danced at parties and sometimes preferred to be
alone and even in an ice cave sometimes and never petulant yet firm
and clear in this until she went home one year and returned as a
blonde then it was never the same, don't try so hard Miss Gallagher
o we love you as you were do not change be like the ice itself and
outlive us all, after all something must and all of our mothers and
most of the fathers have all shown how bad they were

at it so let it be you Miss Gallagher, let it be you

please.

Names

The perfect name for a small dog would be haiku.

My next plane will be named *Lars and the Real Girl*,
not after the movie but after the sex doll in a polyester
after-ski suit sort of like Emma Peel strapped
confidently into the copilot seat.

The dog will ride in a basket between us.

A good name for a bar at McMurdo would be
Rules of Engagement. An ornate bottle opener
in the shape of a naked girl is a rodeo buckle.
Sleep comes in two forms,

tar and china.

Light some smudge pots on top of the hills—
the GPS is dead and the topo map is white paint
on white paper. Prop me up, somebody. Spell words
with spray-painted orange rocks.

Lima Lima Mike Foxtrot:

Army radio code for
lost like a motherfucker. Some days
jink like twitchy bats—some days even
a pawnshop Confederate flag

guitar is not enough.

Whatever my name will be tomorrow
I want to hurry up and learn it soon
just so I can look in the mirror,
practice writing it first with and

then without red lipstick.

Skype

We are arguing about if there are pets
in Heaven and my partner in the miracle
that is marriage assures me that more people
at any moment on earth are dreaming
than are talking, cooking, making love,
or riding bikes. Than are beating dogs,
doing an ollie off a railing, skutching flax,
tightening a wing nut, fixing the photocopier
with a paperclip, or sailing to Byzantium
with SparkNotes and a highlighter. Than
are blowing on tinder to start a fire. More
are dreaming than tying their shoes after
gym. More people right now are dreaming
than are flying, than are driving their cars,
than are pulling all of the triggers on all
of the guns in all of the world. Pulses of joy
and pomegranates fill more dreams than all
the water in all of the Niles rushing over
all the glossy lips to purl into white mist.
There are more dreams than snowflakes,
more dreams than wind, more dreams
than the planets waiting above us for
their turn to come to bed and ravish
the night by kissing the mad circus
horse riders and the drunken pilots
and the dead polar explorers on the
tops of their heads, on their hands,
kissing them right on their wide
mummified sepia mouths.

McMurdo, Still Lucky

One iceberg in a thousand is a black iceberg
and that one usually is me but today must be my day
to be Skittles blessed, and to be blessed among other things
is to walk across the cinder-ash crunch of McMurdo, look down,
and in the path find, stem intact,
with three leaves and no note,

a perfect red plastic
poppy

just waiting to be sewn to the very top
of your best

wool hat.

Pinniped Physiology

                    I remember leaving the handsome one,
the novelist with the tanned body who believed
                    that even our scars could fall in love.
Okay I said. It all turned out really well
                    until it no longer did. Passive and charged
he was some kind of capacitor, silent
                    but latent with current. The time I knew
he could turn it on and off from a black dial
                    was the time I touched him unexpectedly,
and he tensed, pulled away,
                    just the smallest amount. Small but enough
to slap me. I can see him now. He is out there
                    on the ice, one of the seals, because I want him to be fat
and slow and blotchy, and only able to breathe
                    once or twice a day and only when I drag
a circle in the ice and let him come out
                    briefly into the sharp
and surprisingly cold air.
                    The spotting scope pans as I count:
crabeaters doze somewhere, but not here—
                    only Weddell seals wait beside the pressure ridge
not as a pod of, but as a *sausage* of seals.
                    Other kinds more rare. Everything that is known
about the Ross seal (*Ommatophoca rossii*)
                    would fit into a paragraph about half as long
as everything that is confidently known
                    about Sappho. Some things resist completely:
breeding cycles, what causes exile, the triggers
                    for fame and neglect. Do the seals regret land,
want to go back ever to being dogs?

I Cut My Knee, Too

One night I fall down and crick my ankle. I realize I am drunk.
Not drunk with beauty or the sublime or the term *continental drift*

just regular drunk.

It is time to go home.

Exit Interview

"In excitement, a fine, subdued stammering
is interfoliated between regularly spaced whistles."

—Pygmy Owl entry, *Collins Bird Guide*

At McMurdo the NSF Chalet is an
A-frame of certainty and I wonder
is my clicking anything they hear
too but maybe this time I am
the penny that will make the
set complete. Words circle
like horseflies. We know
without even hearing
what the next part
is and still we say
it anyway, often
more than
once.

ACH 044

The portaledge seats again inside the cargo bay,
and it's about damn time. No coffee plus a hard

wind minus the gear we checked in three days ago before
the exit flights all stalled out means that it's fifteen below

an ice cube or something times something Celsius,
windchill rising. I am sitting next to a septic tank-

sized liquid helium vat inside a new C-17 on ACH 044,
return flight to Christchurch. My watch won't move time

from one part of the dial to the other. A dead brother's
brother, alive and less famous, sits next to me. Ice crusts

the chains on the helium tank, not melting. Juice boxes
reject straws. Skin sticks to gloves. I held a meteorite

for hours at the South Pole wrapped in plastic, a baby-
shaped pod of lead, dense as fear. I probably should not

have been allowed to touch it. Somebody says
when are we taking off but I want to know less

about that and more about coming back around:
when will we be standing on the same worn-out carpet

of identical latitude with the baggage circling behind us
while somebody—a wife, a mannequin, a man from

a TV station—says to us, *good job y'all, welcome home, here,
have some gum.* When will it be enough, when will any

of us, even me, say to our childhoods, *bad dog,
go home right now?* We put little pod-buds in our ears

and pretend to sleep. Cold inside the plane. Dark.
What's going on? We are flying home, flying blind,

flying on a wing and a prayer and it's not even a prayer
we know very well. We are flying Antarctica

like the chorky barnstorming wreck that she is.
We are most of us still wearing our Big Reds

but across the left chest, where the white tape
of our name goes, the jackets now all are blank.

I will be you and you can be a meteorite and all of us
can be the kinds of diamonds that once were coal seams

before we taught ourselves to huddle and glow.

Water Sky

Ice blink is the white light seen on the horizon, especially on the underside of low clouds, resulting from reflection of light off a field of ice immediately beyond. It was used by both the Inuit and the explorers looking for the Northwest Passage to help them navigate safely. See also *water sky*.

—from Wikipedia

The blood in my head floats one pulse ahead of the beat, break
dancing like the sound of breaking windows about two houses

down as Janelle Monáe tightropes iPods and my head breaks the sound
barrier just ahead of this C-17 Buck Rogering through space like a dime

store on fire, then something whangs
bad hard

                                —*shit*, what the hell is going on
we all say as the C-17
shimmies to a stop,

        slams open,

fills not with the cool drink of dark beer
on a final hotel balcony New Zealand night

but with hose gushes of hothouse air—
                the plane breaks

open back and front with a hothouse plush of
rotten trash

dead-dogs-and-hot-nights
wet tropical
air.

What the hell.

Cicadas saw like crazy in a Frieda Kahlo antler
light. Swamp bruise.

Blood murk.

No.

We refuse. The Hollow Earth people always said Antarctica was an
entrance to Pellucidar, lost world in the center of the earth, had said
that if you were not careful, about three clouds south-southwest of
Pegasus Field you would some day fly into a sinkhole deeper than a
cyclone inside an oil well and come out the other side of Atlantis. *No.*

Yes.

Whack of knife on wood and we pass around an orchid three, four
times bigger than normal. An even bigger one sags next to it, uncut.
Dragonflies. Steam. We try to find a map, some rope, anything useful.
What the hell. Air sticks to our faces, wet and licking.

Coats off in a red pile. *Anybody got a gun?*

The sky rests on the fingertips of the surrounding trees. Insects
thrum. Mangrove seedlings are already sprouting in a cargo bay
whose fittings have suddenly rusted red and orange, like a row of
oxidized Halloween lights. Were they always that way?

It is—the color is—no, look up, look closer, and the sky seems more
green than blue.

The plane has landed though on something hard, was it the runway once? A sandbar? Where are we. Probe under the moss, or is it crusted seaweed. Most of the concrete has washed away leaving not potholes but tide pools.

In those the water is salty, still warm, like the remnants of an inland sea,

and in the open holes in the runway not jagged gapes like wounds but gardens of coral, curled ledges, topography. *Look,* says the crew chief: *fish.*

Peering into the pools and basins in the street, through the clearing silt warm as spa water, we can see darting schools of blue and tan fish, soft-petaled blossoms of sea anemones, porcupine explosions of purple sea urchins. Oranges and yellows must be sponges, corals, delicate shoots of some delicious ancient seaweed that does not have a name. A baby turquoise crab the size of a quarter rests in the hands of the crew chief who has tasted the water, saying it is good, like the juice of some odd kind of fruit, good but salty, not like table salt but like blood, like the good kind of crying a few days after the funeral when you cry and then hug and are laughing too, all at the same time. The water is clear and warm and we all drink from it and feel different, younger, better. Somebody says parrots are roosting in the tail rudder. Thick clouds wanting to rain have built up and yet the tide pools sparkle with bioluminescence, you can see to walk around them, not fall in, just by their dim green glow. The world is a strange and mysterious place. Miracles happen. In one of the largest tide pools, marine biologists are snorkeling and rising up and down like giddy dolphins until somebody looking for pearls finds a terrace of steps going away down into the darker water. Maybe they had grown in while we were not looking, maybe they had been there all along, nobody is sure. I keep thinking I see somebody I know from home — *there,* just there. We all gather to ease into the water, drawn to the steps with urgency and faith. The longer you stay the easier staying becomes, the better your knees feel, your back, the less interesting air becomes. Some claim they can breathe water as easily as air, except that in comparison, air seems harsh, cold, more like a brittle thing, something that tastes like metal or a kind of cut grass rotting behind a shed.

They are the first.

Walking down the steps, these people motion to others, happy and blurry, excited, swim-walking deeper until lost from view. There is a new life about to start, everybody can feel it—and the line to go in is orderly, everyone polite and laughing, the young ones making a place for the *abuelas*, black men casually holding hands with white men, everybody laughing at the blind man who can now juggle ten oranges at once, people holding up flowers for the parrots to pluck in midflight, all of us ready to go into the water and down the steps, nobody sure what the next life will be only that what is most glorious and interesting is still very much

yet to come.

endnotes

page 7: The Baba Yaga allusion "hut with legs" comes from Lynn Emanuel, *Noose and Hook*.

page 18: *Herc*, a four-engine propeller plane, the LC-130. It lands on skis.

page 25: "Matchbox " originally appeared as prose and in a different order under the title "Orange Crush" in Bill Vaughn's quirky but excellent journal, *The Crunge*.

page 30: "Galen Rowell" lists three Antarctic photographers. Rowell has a book very much worth knowing: *Poles Apart*, pairing northern and southern antipodes. He later died in a plane crash in Bishop. Eliot Porter was the first—before I even knew about Ponting and Hurley, there was in 1978 his coffee table book, *Antarctica*. He had made color nature photography be as important as the black and white of Ansel Adams. Footnote to a footnote is that he was brother to painter Fairfield Porter. For An-My Lê's polar work, see the Web resources sponsored by the Barnard Center for Research on Women, under the work collected as "Gender on Ice."

page 34: "Kate Coles"—this was her idea (and her erasure). It is recycled from her with most kind thanks. Out of vanity I added material back in from the original emails.

page 52: "Pinniped Physiology"—The line about scars falling in love borrows from Galway Kinnell.

page 55: The brothers "ACH 044" references are Mugs and Edmund Stump, both heroes of mine, though for different reasons. Mugs Stump was a climber and mountaineer. Edmund Stump's geology book *The Roof at the Bottom of the World* (2011) came out too late for me to steal anything from, otherwise it would be present here often.

page 57: "Water Sky" perhaps should revert to the original title, "Flying to Pellucidar," in order to honor my NSF grant proposal and, more especially, the father of us all, Edgar Rice Burroughs, inventor of Tarzan and John Carter of Mars and the land of Pellcuidar. Among other things, he was the first writer ever to be incorporated. Born in Chicago, Edgar Rice Burroughs is buried in an unmarked grave in front of a real estate office on Ventura Boulevard, in the San Fernando Valley near Los Angeles. As Gore Vidal says, speaking of the appeal of the *Tarzan* series, we are all heroes of our own movies.

acknowledgments

Thank you: Kevin Bryan, Jared Burton, the Byrd Polar Research Center, Gary Cardullo, Matt Coolidge, Chris Cokinos, Kate Coles — and even though she was just listed she deserves a second mention, so Kate Coles, Jesse Crain, Ian Dalziel, Bodie Davies, Jordan Davis, Nicelle Davis, Tonya Edwards, Sam Feola, Bill Fox, Kate Gale, Mike Guista, Mark Hoffer, Abbey Fitting Hood, Amber Hood, Elaine Hood (no relation, but we do have very similar birthdays), Patricia Jackson, Matthew Jaffe, Karen Joyce, Maria Maggi, Karen Moore, Christine Mugnolo, Joan Myers, the National Science Foundation, David Nelson, Cheryl Parker, PHI, Inc. and the staff thereof, Peter Rejcek, the Scott Polar Research Institute, Rae Spain, Santi Tafarella, Sharon Taylor, Annette Valle, Bill Vaughn, Nick West, Mike Wilson, and the Artists & Writers Program Director, Peter West.

At Ohio University Press, thank you goes as well to Nancy Basmajian, Kevin Haworth, Beth Pratt, and Sarah Welsch.

"You'll live to write a book about it."

—One pilot to another, about risking a flight to the South Pole, Frank Capra, *Dirigible*, 1931